SISTER CRISTINA PITTS

Meditations for Lent 2024

A 40-Day Devotional with Reflections, Actions, and Daily Prayers for Holy Week and Easter

Contents

Introduction

Greetings on this sacred journey of Lenten reflection and spiritual growth. As we embark on these forty days of purposeful introspection, let us create space in our hearts for the transformative work of God. This devotional is a companion on your pilgrimage, inviting you to delve deeper into the significance of Lent and discover the purpose it holds for your faith journey.

Lent, a season of forty days, echoes the forty days Jesus spent in the wilderness. It's a time of intentional self-reflection, a spiritual retreat where we engage in prayer, fasting, and acts of kindness. This intentional focus allows us to draw nearer to God, aligning our hearts with His purpose.

Overview of Lent

Lent is more than a liturgical season; it is a sacred interval for believers to emulate Christ's journey toward the cross. It begins on Ash Wednesday and concludes on Easter Sunday, encompassing the Passion, death, and resurrection of Jesus. This period of self-examination and penance encourages us to reevaluate our lives, deepen our connection with God, and grow in spiritual maturity.

The wilderness experience of Lent is an opportunity to confront our vulnerabilities, just as Jesus faced temptations in the desert. It's not about mere deprivation but a deliberate effort to prioritize the eternal over the temporal. Through prayer, we seek divine guidance; through fasting, we cultivate self-discipline, and through acts of kindness, we share God's love with others.

Purpose of the Devotional

This devotional is curated to enrich your Lenten experience. It is designed as a daily guide, offering reflections, actions, and prayers to accompany you on this journey of spiritual renewal. The intention is not to prescribe a rigid set of rules but to create a space for personal encounters with God's Word and His transformative grace.

As you engage with the devotional content, may it serve as a beacon, illuminating the path of spiritual growth and fostering a deeper connection with God. Embrace each day as an opportunity to draw nearer to the heart of Christ, allowing the insights and prompts to inspire your reflections and prayers.

1

Ash Wednesday to Saturday

Day 1: Ash Wednesday - Embracing Reflection

Scripture:

"Joel 2:12 - 'Yet even now,' declares the Lord, 'return to me with all your heart, with fasting, with weeping, and with mourning.'"

Inspiration:

On this Ash Wednesday, let us turn our hearts back to the Lord with sincerity. As we receive the ashes, may they symbolize not only our mortality but our willingness to embrace reflection. This day marks the beginning of a sacred journey inward, an opportunity to assess our lives in the light of God's grace.

Quote:

"Ashes are not an end but a beginning - a call to repentance, a sign of God's mercy, and an invitation to new life." - Unknown

Prayer:

Lord, as we carry the ashes, may they be a reminder of our humble state and a catalyst for genuine reflection. Guide us on this Lenten journey, as we return to You with all our hearts. Amen.

Day 2: Thursday in the First Week - Contemplating Change

Scripture:

"2 Corinthians 5:17 - Therefore, if anyone is in Christ, he is a new creation. The old has passed away; behold, the new has come."

Inspiration:

As we contemplate change, remember that in Christ, we are made new. The first step toward spiritual renewal is acknowledging our need for transformation. Today, open your heart to the possibility of becoming a new creation in Christ.

Quote:

"Change is not something to fear; it's the process of becoming who God created you to be." - Rick Warren

Prayer:

Heavenly Father, grant us the courage to embrace the changes You desire for us. May we surrender to Your transformative power, becoming new creations in Christ. Amen.

Day 3: Friday in the First Week - Fasting and Prayer

Scripture:

"Matthew 6:16-18 - And when you fast, do not look gloomy like the hypocrites, for they disfigure their faces that their fasting may be seen by others. Truly, I say to you, they have received their reward. But when you fast, anoint your head and wash your face, that your fasting may not be seen by others but by your Father who is in secret."

Inspiration:

Fasting and prayer are not meant for show but for a deepened connection with God. Today, as you fast, let it be a personal offering to the Father in secret. May your hunger be a reminder of dependence on Him.

Quote:

"Fasting is a powerful spiritual discipline that redirects our focus from the physical to the spiritual." - Unknown

Prayer:

Lord, as we fast and pray, may our hearts be tuned to Your presence. May this act of self-denial draw us closer to You, seeking Your will above all else. Amen.

Day 4: Saturday in the First Week - Seeking Spiritual Growth

Scripture:

"Colossians 2:6-7 - Therefore, as you received Christ Jesus the Lord, so walk in him, rooted and built up in him and established in the faith, just as you were taught, abounding in thanksgiving."

Inspiration:

On this Saturday, seek spiritual growth by rooting yourself in Christ. Let your faith be a wellspring, nourishing the soil of your soul. As you grow in Him, may thanksgiving overflow from your heart.

Quote:

"Spiritual growth is a journey, not a destination. It's about becoming more like Christ each day." - Billy Graham

Prayer:

Gracious God, as we seek spiritual growth, may our roots go deep into the soil of Your love. Establish us in faith, and let gratitude abound in our hearts. In Jesus' name, we pray. Amen.

2

Ash Wednesday to Saturday: Self-Reflection

How can the ashes of repentance pave the way for new growth in your spiritual garden?

3

Week 1

Day 1: Monday - Setting Intentions

Scripture:

"Proverbs 16:3 - Commit your work to the Lord, and your plans will be established."

Inspiration:

On this Monday, let us set our intentions before the Lord. As we commit our plans to Him, may our actions align with His will. Invite God into your day, seeking His guidance in all you do.

Quote:

"Setting intentions is like drawing a map for your life – let God be the compass." - Unknown

Prayer:

Heavenly Father, guide us as we set our intentions before You. May our plans be established by Your perfect will. Amen.

Day 2: Tuesday - Embracing Silence

Scripture:

"Psalm 46:10 - Be still, and know that I am God. I will be exalted among the nations; I will be exalted in the earth."

Inspiration:

In the silence of this Tuesday, embrace the presence of God. Be still and recognize His sovereignty. In the quiet, His voice is heard, bringing peace and assurance.

Quote:

"Silence is a language only the soul understands; it is where God speaks most profoundly." - Brennan Manning

Prayer:

Lord, as we embrace the silence, may we profoundly encounter You. Speak to our hearts and bring a deep sense of peace. Amen.

Day 3: Wednesday - Acts of Kindness

Scripture:

"Ephesians 4:32 - Be kind to one another, tenderhearted, forgiving one another, as God in Christ forgave you."

Inspiration:

On this Wednesday, let acts of kindness flow from your heart. In forgiving and showing compassion, reflect the kindness God has shown you. Your actions can be a tangible expression of His love.

Quote:

"Kindness is the language that the deaf can hear and the blind can see." - Mark Twain

Prayer:

Loving God, help us extend kindness to others as a reflection of Your boundless love. May our actions be a testimony to Your grace. Amen.

Day 4: Thursday - Repentance and Forgiveness

Scripture:

"*1 John 1:9 - If we confess our sins, he is faithful and just to forgive us our sins and to cleanse us from all unrighteousness.*"

Inspiration:

Thursday calls us to repentance and forgiveness. Confess your sins before God, and embrace the cleansing power of His forgiveness. Extend this grace to others as well.

Quote:

"*Repentance is not just turning away from sin; it's turning toward God.*" - Billy Graham

Prayer:

Merciful Father, as we repent and seek Your forgiveness, cleanse us from all unrighteousness. Grant us the strength to forgive others as You have forgiven us. Amen.

Day 5: Friday - Reflection on Sacrifice

Scripture:

"*Romans 12:1 - I appeal to you therefore, brothers, by the mercies of God, to present your bodies as a living sacrifice, holy and acceptable to God, which is your spiritual worship.*"

Inspiration:

Reflect on the sacrifice Christ made for us. As we offer our lives as living sacrifices, may our actions be a form of worship, pleasing to God.

Quote:

"Sacrifice is the language of love, and love is the currency of the kingdom." - Ann Voskamp

Prayer:

Lord, as we reflect on sacrifice, may our lives be offerings of worship to You. Help us understand the depth of Your love demonstrated on the cross. Amen.

Day 6: Saturday - Renewing Faith

Scripture:

"Hebrews 11:1 - Now faith is the assurance of things hoped for, the conviction of things not seen."

Inspiration:

On this Saturday, renew your faith in the unseen promises of God. Trust in His faithfulness, and let hope be the anchor for your soul.

Quote:

"Faith is taking the first step even when you don't see the whole staircase." - Martin Luther King Jr.

Prayer:

Faithful God, renew our faith in You. May we find assurance in Your promises, even when we cannot see the outcome? Strengthen our conviction in the unseen. Amen.

4

Week 1: Self-Reflection

What stood out to you this week?

5

Week 2

Day 1: Monday - Gratitude in the Journey

Scripture:

"1 Thessalonians 5:18 - Give thanks in all circumstances; for this is the will of God in Christ Jesus for you."

Inspiration:

Begin this week with a heart of gratitude. In every step of your journey, give thanks. Gratitude shifts our perspective, aligning our hearts with God's will.

Quote:

"Gratitude unlocks the fullness of life. It turns what we have into enough." - Melody Beattie

Prayer:

Heavenly Father, we express gratitude for the journey You've set before us. Help us cultivate thankful hearts, recognizing Your presence in every circumstance. Amen.

Day 2: Tuesday - Temptations and Resilience

Scripture:

"1 Corinthians 10:13 - No temptation has overtaken you that is not common to man. God is faithful, and he will not let you be tempted beyond your ability, but with the temptation, he will also provide the way of escape, that you may be able to endure it."

Inspiration:

In the face of temptations, remember God's faithfulness. He provides strength for resilience. Stand firm, knowing you are not alone in the struggle.

Quote:

"Resilience is not about being strong but about being able to bounce back." - Unknown

Prayer:

Lord, in times of temptation, grant us the strength to endure. May we find refuge in Your faithfulness and the resilience to overcome. Amen.

Day 3: Wednesday - Compassion for Others

Scripture:

"Colossians 3:12 - Put on then, as God's chosen ones, holy and beloved, compassionate hearts, kindness, humility, meekness, and patience."

Inspiration:

Wednesday calls us to don compassionate hearts. Let kindness and humility guide your interactions. In showing compassion, we mirror the heart of God.

Quote:

"Compassion is the key to unlocking the door of a closed heart." - Unknown

Prayer:

Loving God, help us put on compassionate hearts. May our actions reflect Your kindness and humility, bringing Your love to those around us. Amen.

Day 4: Thursday - Deepening Prayer Life

Scripture:

"Philippians 4:6-7 - Do not be anxious about anything, but in everything by prayer and supplication with thanksgiving, let your requests be made known to God. And the peace of God, which

surpasses all understanding, will guard your hearts and your minds in Christ Jesus."

Inspiration:

Deepen your prayer life this Thursday. Bring your anxieties and requests before God. In prayer, find the peace that surpasses understanding.

Quote:

"Prayer is not asking. It is a longing of the soul." - Mahatma Gandhi

Prayer:

Heavenly Father, as we deepen our prayer life, may Your peace guard our hearts and minds. In every supplication, may we draw closer to You. Amen.

Day 5: Friday - Letting Go of Attachments

Scripture:

"Matthew 6:19-21 - Do not lay up for yourselves treasures on earth, where moth and rust destroy and where thieves break in and steal, but lay up for yourselves treasures in heaven, where neither moth nor rust destroys and where thieves do not break in and steal. For where your treasure is, there your heart will be also."

Inspiration:

Friday prompts us to let go of earthly attachments. Invest in heavenly treasures, for where your treasure is, there your heart will be also.

Quote:

"Letting go doesn't mean giving up, but rather accepting that there are things that cannot be." - Unknown

Prayer:

Lord, help us release earthly attachments and fix our hearts on heavenly treasures. May our priorities align with Your eternal purposes. Amen.

Day 6: Saturday - Connecting with Community

Scripture:

"Hebrews 10:24-25 - And let us consider how to stir up one another to love and good works, not neglecting to meet together, as is the habit of some, but encouraging one another, and all the more as you see the Day drawing near."

Inspiration:

On this Saturday, connect with your community. Encourage one another in love and good works. Together, we find strength for the journey.

Quote:

"Community is where humility and glory touch." - Henri Nouwen

Prayer:

Gracious God, helps us foster connections within our community. May we uplift and encourage one another, drawing strength from our shared journey of faith. Amen.

6

Week 2: Self-Reflection

**What are you thankful for, and how can sacrificial love
impact your relationships?**

7

Week 3

Day 1: Monday - Patience in Waiting

Scripture:

"Psalm 27:14 - Wait for the Lord; be strong, and let your heart take courage; wait for the Lord!"

Inspiration:

Monday calls for patience in waiting. As we wait upon the Lord, let our hearts take courage, knowing that His timing is perfect.

Quote:

"Patience is not the ability to wait but the ability to keep a good attitude while waiting." - Joyce Meyer

Prayer:

Lord, grant us patience as we wait for Your guidance. Strengthen our hearts, and may we find courage in the assurance of Your perfect timing. Amen.

Day 2: Tuesday - Humility and Self-Reflection

Scripture:

"James 4:10 - Humble yourselves before the Lord, and he will exalt you."

Inspiration:

Tuesday prompts humility and self-reflection. As we humble ourselves before the Lord, may His grace exalt us in due time.

Quote:

"Humility is not thinking less of yourself; it's thinking of yourself less." - C.S. Lewis

Prayer:

Heavenly Father, help us cultivate humility in our hearts. May our self-reflection lead to a deeper understanding of Your grace. Amen.

Day 3: Wednesday - Acts of Charity

Scripture:

"Galatians 6:2 - Bear one another's burdens, and so fulfill the law of Christ."

Inspiration:

Wednesday calls us to acts of charity. Let us bear one another's burdens, fulfilling the law of Christ through love and compassion.

Quote:

"Charity sees the need, not the cause." - German Proverb

Prayer:

Lord, guide us to bear the burdens of others with love. May our acts of charity be a reflection of Your boundless compassion. Amen.

Day 4: Thursday - Seeking Guidance

Scripture:

"Proverbs 3:5-6 - Trust in the Lord with all your heart, and do not lean on your understanding. In all your ways acknowledge him, and he will make straight your paths."

Inspiration:

Thursday prompts us to seek guidance from the Lord. Trust in His wisdom and acknowledge Him in all your ways, and He will make your paths straight.

Quote:

"God's guidance is like a GPS for the soul; trust the journey even when you don't understand the route." - Unknown

Prayer:

Loving God, guide us in seeking Your wisdom and acknowledging Your presence in our lives. May our paths be straightened by Your divine guidance. Amen.

Day 5: Friday - Nurturing Spiritual Discipline

Scripture:

"1 Timothy 4:7-8 - Have nothing to do with irreverent, silly myths. Rather train yourself for godliness; for while bodily training is of some value, godliness is of value in every way, as it holds promise for the present life and also for the life to come."

Inspiration:

Friday urges us to nurture spiritual discipline. Train yourself for godliness, recognizing its value both in this life and in the life to come.

Quote:

"Spiritual disciplines are not a way to earn God's love; they are a way to respond to it." - Richard J. Foster

Prayer:

Lord, help us cultivate spiritual discipline in our lives. May our efforts lead to godliness and align us with Your eternal promises. Amen.

Day 6: Saturday - Reconciliation with Others

Scripture:

"Matthew 5:23-24 - So if you are offering your gift at the altar and there remember that your brother has something against you, leave your gift there before the altar and go. First, be reconciled to your brother, and then come and offer your gift."

Inspiration:

Saturday emphasizes reconciliation with others. Before presenting our gifts to God, let us seek reconciliation with those we may have offended.

Quote:

"Reconciliation is not about being right; it's about restoring relationships." - Unknown

Prayer:

Gracious Father, grant us the humility to seek reconciliation with others. May our hearts be open to healing, mirroring Your grace in our relationships. Amen.

8

Week 3: Self-Reflection

How have these virtues shaped your interactions?

9

Week 4

Day 1: Monday - Examining Inner Motivations

Scripture:

"Psalm 139:23-24 - Search me, O God, and know my heart! Try me and know my thoughts! And see if there be any grievous way in me, and lead me in the way everlasting."

Inspiration:

Monday prompts us to examine inner motivations. Invite God to search your heart, revealing any areas that need His transformative touch. Surrender to His leading in the everlasting way.

Quote:

"Inner renewal starts with an honest examination of our hearts in the light of God's truth." - Unknown

Prayer:

Lord, as we examine our inner motivations, search our hearts, and lead us in the way everlasting. May our thoughts align with Your truth. Amen.

Day 2: Tuesday - Cultivating Joy

Scripture:

"Psalm 16:11 - You make known to me the path of life; in your presence, there is fullness of joy; at your right hand are pleasures forevermore."

Inspiration:

Tuesday calls for cultivating joy. In God's presence, find the fullness of joy that transcends circumstances. Allow His joy to be your strength.

Quote:

"Joy is the echo of God's life within us." - Columba of Iona

Prayer:

Heavenly Father, cultivate joy in our hearts. May we find delight in Your presence and draw strength from the joy that comes from knowing You. Amen.

Day 3: Wednesday - Healing Brokenness

Scripture:

"Isaiah 53:5 - But he was pierced for our transgressions; he was crushed for our iniquities; upon him was the chastisement that brought us peace, and with his wounds, we are healed."

Inspiration:

Wednesday focuses on healing brokenness. Remember the sacrifice of Christ, whose wounds bring us healing and peace. Surrender brokenness to the One who restores.

Quote:

"Healing may not be so much about getting better as about letting go of everything that isn't you." - Rachel Naomi Remen

Prayer:

Lord Jesus, with gratitude, we acknowledge Your sacrifice for our healing. Mend our brokenness and bring peace to our hearts. Amen.

Day 4: Thursday - Grappling with Suffering

Scripture:

"Romans 8:18 - For I consider that the sufferings of this present time are not worth comparing with the glory that is to be revealed to us."

Inspiration:

Thursday grapples with suffering. Amid trials, remember that the glory to come far surpasses present struggles. Endure with hope.

Quote:

"Suffering is not an obstacle to be overcome but a path to be walked with Christ." - Unknown

Prayer:

Lord, in times of suffering, grant us strength and perseverance. May we walk the path with You, knowing that glory awaits us. Amen.

Day 5: Friday - Cultivating Generosity

Scripture:

"2 Corinthians 9:7 - Each one must give as he has decided in his heart, not reluctantly or under compulsion, for God loves a cheerful giver."

Inspiration:

Friday encourages cultivating generosity. Give with a cheerful heart, reflecting God's love. Generosity is a joyful response to His abundant grace.

Quote:

"Generosity is not about how much you have but how much you are willing to give." - Unknown

Prayer:

Gracious God, teach us to cultivate generosity in our lives. May our giving be a cheerful reflection of Your abundant love. Amen.

Day 6: Saturday - Strengthening Faith

Scripture:

"Hebrews 11:1 - Now faith is the assurance of things hoped for, the conviction of things not seen."

Inspiration:

Saturday is about strengthening faith. Have faith, trusting in the assurance of things hoped for and the conviction of things not seen. Walk confidently in God's promises.

Quote:

"Faith is not the absence of doubt but the courage to embrace uncertainty." - Unknown

Prayer:

Lord, strengthen our faith. May we walk with confidence in Your promises, even when we cannot see the outcome. Amen.

10

Week 4: Self-Reflection

**What motivations guide your actions, and how can
acknowledging brokenness lead to healing?**

11

Week 5

Day 1: Monday - Embracing Simplicity

Scripture:

"Matthew 6:33 - But seek first the kingdom of God and his righteousness, and all these things will be added to you."

Inspiration:

Monday calls for embracing simplicity. Seek the kingdom of God above all else, finding contentment in His righteousness. In simplicity, discover the richness of His provision.

Quote:

"Simplicity is the ultimate sophistication." - Leonardo da Vinci

Prayer:

Heavenly Father, help us embrace simplicity in our lives. May our focus be on Your kingdom, finding fulfillment in Your righteousness. Amen.

Day 2: Tuesday - Finding Beauty in the Ordinary

Scripture:

"Psalm 118:24 - This is the day that the Lord has made; let us rejoice and be glad in it."

Inspiration:

Tuesday invites us to find beauty in the ordinary. Rejoice in each day the Lord has made, recognizing the extraordinary in the simplicity of His creation.

Quote:

"In every walk with nature, one receives far more than he seeks." - John Muir

Prayer:

Lord, open our eyes to the beauty in the ordinary. May we find joy in the simplicity of Your creation and rejoice in each day You have made. Amen.

Day 3: Wednesday - Resisting Distractions

Scripture:

"Colossians 3:2 - Set your minds on things that are above, not on things that are on earth."

Inspiration:

Wednesday calls for resisting distractions. Set your mind on heavenly things, avoiding the noise of earthly distractions. In focus, find spiritual clarity.

Quote:

"Distractions are the enemy of wisdom." - Shane Parrish

Prayer:

Lord, help us resist distractions and fix our minds on things above. May our focus be unwavering as we seek Your wisdom and guidance. Amen.

Day 4: Thursday - Cultivating Stillness

Scripture:

"Psalm 46:10 - Be still, and know that I am God. I will be exalted among the nations; I will be exalted in the earth."

Inspiration:

Thursday prompts cultivating stillness. Be still and know that God is exalted. In the quiet, hear His voice and find solace in His presence.

Quote:

"Silence is the language of God; all else is poor translation." - Rumi

Prayer:

Heavenly Father, in the stillness, may we know You are God. Let Your presence fill the quiet spaces, bringing peace to our hearts. Amen.

Day 5: Friday - Embodying Love

Scripture:

"1 Corinthians 16:14 - Let all that you do be done in love."

Inspiration:

Friday encourages embodying love. In all your actions, let love be the driving force. Reflect on the love of Christ in your interactions with others.

Quote:

"Love is not just something you feel; it's something you do." - David Wilkerson

Prayer:

Lord, may all that we do be done in love. Help us embody Your love in our words and actions, reflecting Your grace to those around us. Amen.

Day 6: Saturday - Rejoicing in Progress

Scripture:

"Philippians 1:6 - And I am sure of this, that he who began a good work in you will bring it to completion at the day of Jesus Christ."

Inspiration:

Saturday invites rejoicing in progress. Trust that God, who began a good work in you, will bring it to completion. Celebrate the journey of growth and transformation.

Quote:

"Progress is not in the destination but in the journey." - Unknown

Prayer:

Gracious God, thank you for the progress You've brought into our lives. May we rejoice in the journey, trusting in Your ongoing work of transformation. Amen.

12

Week 5: Self-Reflection

How can simplicity enhance your spiritual life?

13

Holy Week

Day 1: Palm Sunday - Welcoming Transformation

Scripture:

"Psalm 51:10 - Create in me a clean heart, O God, and renew a right spirit within me."

Inspiration:

Palm Sunday invites us to welcome transformation. As we celebrate Christ's triumphal entry, let us open our hearts for God's renewing work, creating in us a spirit aligned with His righteousness.

Quote:

"The palm branch signifies victory, triumph, peace, and eternal life—gifts Christ brought us." - Unknown

Prayer:

Lord, on this Palm Sunday, create in us clean hearts and renew the right spirits within us. May we welcome the transformative power of Your grace. Amen.

Day 2: Monday of Holy Week - Reflection on Servanthood

Scripture:

"Mark 10:45 - For even the Son of Man came not to be served but to serve, and to give his life as a ransom for many."

Inspiration:

Monday of Holy Week calls for reflection on servanthood. As Jesus humbly served, may we also seek opportunities to serve others, embodying the selfless love of our Savior.

Quote:

"True greatness is not found in how much you can get, but in how much you can give." - Unknown

Prayer:

Heavenly Father, help us reflect on the example of Jesus, who came to serve. May we find joy in serving others, mirroring His sacrificial love. Amen.

Day 3: Tuesday of Holy Week - The Last Supper

Scripture:

"Luke 22:19-20 - And he took bread, and when he had given thanks, he broke it and gave it to them, saying, 'This is my body, which is given for you. Do this in remembrance of me.' And likewise, the cup after they had eaten, saying, 'This cup that is poured out for you is the new covenant in my blood.'"

Inspiration:

Tuesday of Holy Week reflects on the Last Supper. Commemorate this sacred moment, remembering Christ's body broken and His blood shed for the forgiveness of sins. Partake in communion with reverence and gratitude.

Quote:

"The Last Supper was not the end; it was the beginning of a new covenant sealed with the precious blood of Jesus." - Unknown

Prayer:

Lord, as we remember the Last Supper, we partake in communion with reverence. Thank you for the new covenant sealed by the sacrifice of Your Son. Amen.

Day 4: Wednesday of Holy Week - Betrayal and Forgiveness

Scripture:

"Matthew 26:41 - Watch and pray that you may not enter into temptation. The spirit indeed is willing, but the flesh is weak."

Inspiration:

Wednesday of Holy Week acknowledges betrayal and forgiveness. Reflect on the weakness of the flesh and the need for vigilance in prayer. Embrace the grace of forgiveness, mirroring Christ's mercy.

Quote:

"Forgiveness is the fragrance that the violet sheds on the heel that has crushed it." - Mark Twain

Prayer:

Gracious God, on this Wednesday, grants us strength to resist temptation. Help us forgive as we've been forgiven and extend mercy to those who may betray us. Amen.

Day 5: Maundy Thursday - Washing Feet, Sharing Grace

Scripture:

"John 13:14-15 - If I then, your Lord and Teacher, have washed your feet, you also ought to wash one another's feet. For I have given you an example, that you also should do just as I have done to you."

Inspiration:

Maundy Thursday exemplifies washing feet and sharing grace. Follow Christ's example of humble service and grace, fostering a spirit of love and unity.

Quote:

"In serving others, we find the essence of Christ's command to love one another." - Unknown

Prayer:

Lord, as we recall the foot-washing on Maundy Thursday, inspire us to serve one another with humility and extend Your grace to those around us. Amen.

Day 6: Good Friday - The Cross and Redemption

Scripture:

"Isaiah 53:5 - But he was pierced for our transgressions; he was crushed for our iniquities; upon him was the chastisement that brought us peace, and with his wounds, we are healed."

Inspiration:

Good Friday reflects on the cross and redemption. Contemplate the depth of Christ's sacrifice, recognizing that His wounds bring us healing and peace.

Quote:

"The cross is the epitome of sacrificial love—where mercy and justice embrace." - Unknown

Prayer:

Lord Jesus, on this Good Friday, we contemplate the profound sacrifice of the cross. Thank you for the redemption and healing found in Your wounds. Amen.

Day 7: Holy Saturday - Waiting in Hope

Scripture:

"Lamentations 3:24 - 'The Lord is my portion,' says my soul, 'therefore I will hope in him.'"

Inspiration:

Holy Saturday encourages waiting in hope. Amidst the silence, trust in the Lord as your portion. Find hope in His promises, anticipating the joy of resurrection.

Quote:

"In the stillness of Holy Saturday, hope quietly prepares for the joy of Easter morning." - Unknown

Prayer:

Heavenly Father, on this Holy Saturday, our souls declare that You are our portion. May we wait in hope, trusting in Your promises and anticipating the joy of resurrection. Amen.

14

Holy Week: Self-Reflection

How have these reflections deepened your understanding of Christ's sacrifice?

15

Easter Week:

Day 1: Easter Sunday - Resurrection Celebration

Scripture:

"1 Corinthians 15:55 - 'O death, where is your victory? O death, where is your sting?'"

Inspiration:

Easter Sunday marks the Resurrection Celebration. Rejoice in the victory over death through Christ's resurrection. His triumph removes the sting of death, offering eternal life.

Quote:

"The resurrection gives my life meaning and direction and the opportunity to start over no matter what my circumstances." - Robert Flatt

Prayer:

Lord, on this Easter Sunday, we celebrate the victory over death. Thank you for the hope and new life found in the resurrection of Your Son, Jesus Christ. Amen.

Day 2: Monday after Easter - Living in the Light

Scripture:

"1 John 1:7 - But if we walk in the light, as he is in the light, we have fellowship with one another, and the blood of Jesus his Son cleanses us from all sin."

Inspiration:

The Monday after Easter calls us to live in the light. Walk in fellowship with God and others, knowing that the blood of Jesus cleanses us from all sin.

Quote:

"Living in the light means transparency, authenticity, and an unwavering commitment to truth." - Unknown

Prayer:

Heavenly Father, help us walk in the light as You are in the light. May our lives reflect transparency, authenticity, and a commitment to truth through the cleansing power of Jesus' blood. Amen.

Day 3: Tuesday after Easter - Continuing Transformation

Scripture:

"2 Corinthians 3:18 - And we all, with unveiled face, beholding the glory of the Lord, are being transformed into the same image from one degree of glory to another. For this comes from the Lord who is the Spirit."

Inspiration:

Tuesday after Easter prompts us to continue the transformation. Behold the glory of the Lord, allowing His Spirit to mold us into His image, progressing from one degree of glory to another.

Quote:

"Transformation is a journey, not a destination, and it requires ongoing surrender to the guiding hand of the Holy Spirit." - Unknown

Prayer:

Lord, as we behold Your glory, continue the transformation process in our lives. Guide us through this ongoing journey of becoming more like You. Amen.

Day 4: Wednesday after Easter - A New Beginning

Scripture:

"2 Corinthians 5:17 - Therefore, if anyone is in Christ, he is a new creation. The old has passed away; behold, the new has come."

Inspiration:

Wednesday after Easter signifies a new beginning. In Christ, we are made new. Embrace the transformative power that comes from being a new creation in Him.

Quote:

"Every sunrise is God's way of saying, 'Let's start again.'" - Todd Stocker

Prayer:

Gracious God, thank you for the new beginning we have in Christ. May we embrace the freshness of each day, knowing that we are a new creation in Him. Amen.

Day 5: Thursday after Easter - Sharing the Joy

Scripture:

"Psalm 105:3 - Glory in his holy name; let the hearts of those who seek the Lord rejoice!"

Inspiration:

Thursday after Easter encourages us to share the joy. Rejoice in the holy name of the Lord, and let your heart overflow with joy as you share the Good News with others.

Quote:

"Joy is the infallible sign of the presence of God." - Pierre Teilhard de Chardin

Prayer:

Lord, may our hearts rejoice in Your holy name. Help us share the joy that comes from knowing You with those around us. Amen.

Day 6: Friday after Easter - Reflecting on Renewal

Scripture:

"Romans 12:2 - Do not be conformed to this world, but be transformed by the renewal of your mind, that by testing you may discern what is the will of God, what is good and acceptable and perfect."

Inspiration:

Friday after Easter prompts reflection on renewal. Resist conformity to the world and allow your mind to be renewed by God's transformative power, discerning His will.

Quote:

"Renewal is not just about changing circumstances; it's about transforming perspectives and aligning with God's perfect will." - Unknown

Prayer:

Heavenly Father, renew our minds and transform our perspectives. May we discern Your perfect will and align ourselves with what is good, acceptable, and perfect. Amen.

Day 7: Saturday after Easter - Sustaining the Journey

Scripture:

"Isaiah 40:31 - but they who wait for the Lord shall renew their strength; they shall mount up with wings like eagles; they shall run and not be weary; they shall walk and not faint."

Inspiration:

Saturday after Easter encourages us to sustain the journey. Wait upon the Lord, renew your strength, and continue the journey with the endurance that comes from Him.

Quote:

"Sustaining the journey requires patience, trust, and reliance on the strength that comes from waiting on the Lord." - Unknown

Prayer:

Lord, as we wait upon You, renew our strength. May we soar with eagles' wings, run without weariness, and walk without fainting, sustained by Your grace. Amen.

16

Easter Week: Self-Reflection

What impact does the risen Christ have on your life?

17

Conclusion

In the tapestry of spiritual renewal woven through the days of Lent, Holy Week, and Easter, we've embarked on a transformative journey. From introspective reflections to the joyous celebration of Christ's resurrection, each day has been an invitation to draw closer to God, embrace change, and live in the light of His grace.

As we conclude this devotional journey, let us carry the lessons learned into the days that follow. May the themes of repentance, sacrifice, service, and renewal continue to resonate in our hearts. Let the rhythms of prayer, scripture, and reflection be the melody that shapes our daily lives.

Remember, spiritual renewal is an ongoing process—a journey with Christ that extends beyond the pages of this devotional. May we walk in the assurance of God's love, embody the transformative power of His Word, and share the joy of our salvation with a world in need.

May the grace of our Lord Jesus Christ, the love of God, and the fellowship of the Holy Spirit be with us now and always.

Amen.

Printed in Great Britain
by Amazon

37221273R00046